To my loving mom, my first teacher, for giving me
the skills that made me what I am today. — J.V.C.

To my grandmother, Imogene Gaylor, with love. — J.P.

Publish-a-Book is a trademark of Steck-Vaughn Company.

Copyright © 1997 Steck-Vaughn Company.

Printed in the United States of America.

1 2 3 4 5 6 7 8 9 0   IP   01 00 99 98 97 96

Library of Congress Cataloging-in-Publication Data

Cann, Jonathan V., 1983 –
    The case of the crooked candles / story by Jonathan V. Cann; illustrations by Jean Pidgeon.
      p.   cm. — (Publish-a-book)
    Summary: Detective Dog and his animal assistants help keep their small New Jersey town safe from crime by tracking down some pesky thieves.
    ISBN 0–8172–4432–8
    1. Children's writings, American. [1. Animals — Fiction. 2. Mystery and detective stories. 3. Children's writings.] I. Pidgeon, Jean, ill. II. Title. III. Series.
PZ7.C168Cas 1997
[Fic]—dc20

96-44842
CIP AC

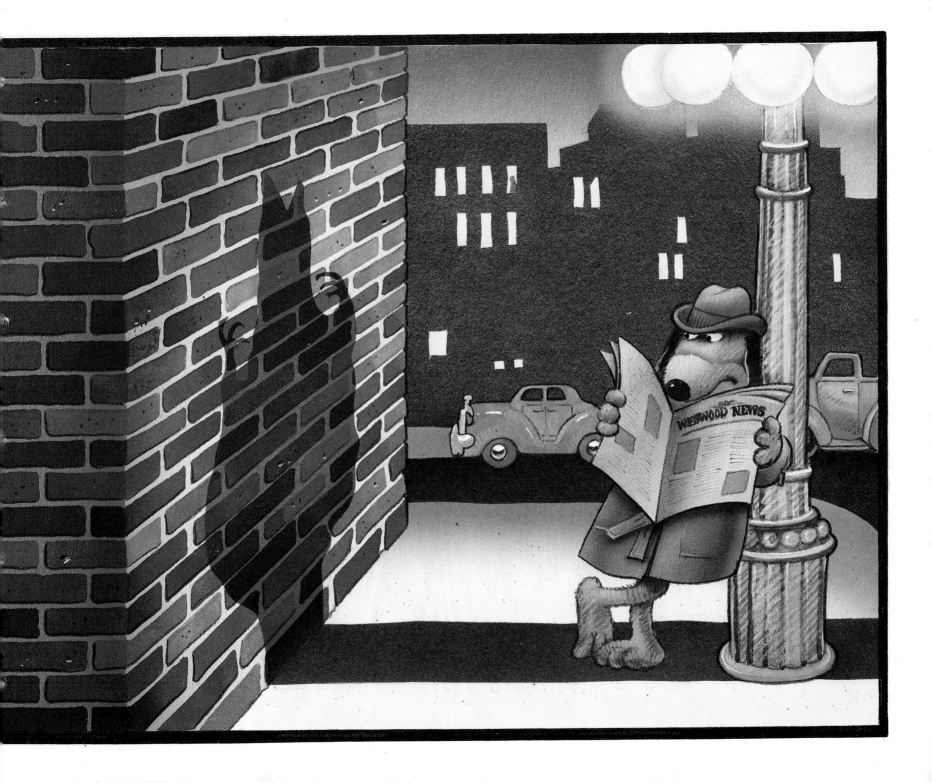

Many people who come to the small town of Westwood, New Jersey, ask, "Why is this the only town in the area that has a nearly spotless solution and conviction record when it comes to crime?" The town officials' answer is always the same, "It's because of the Detective Dog Team!"

Of course, most people have no idea what these officials are talking about. That is, they have no idea until a villain tries to commit a crime.

The Detective Dog Team is the finest band of crime solvers Westwood has ever had. Detective Dog is a freelance sleuth who investigates every bit of foul play he encounters. Craig Frog loves to hop about and explore his surroundings. Jon Mouse is a talented inventor who can fit into small nooks and crannies. Chris Duck has perfected his flying, and can now outfly some vehicles. Ned Cat has learned how to pick locks with his sharp claws. Last but not least, Matthew Spider has the strongest, firmest webbing you have ever seen.

These crack detectives and their special abilities have solved many cases together. This is the story of one of their crowning achievements: "The Case of the Crooked Candles."

When the cry rang out from Parian Jewelers, people all over town heard it loud and clear.

"Help! Police! I've been robbed!" The cry for help came from Ben Ruby, the owner of Parian Jewelers.

The Detective Dog Team was on the scene long before the police arrived.

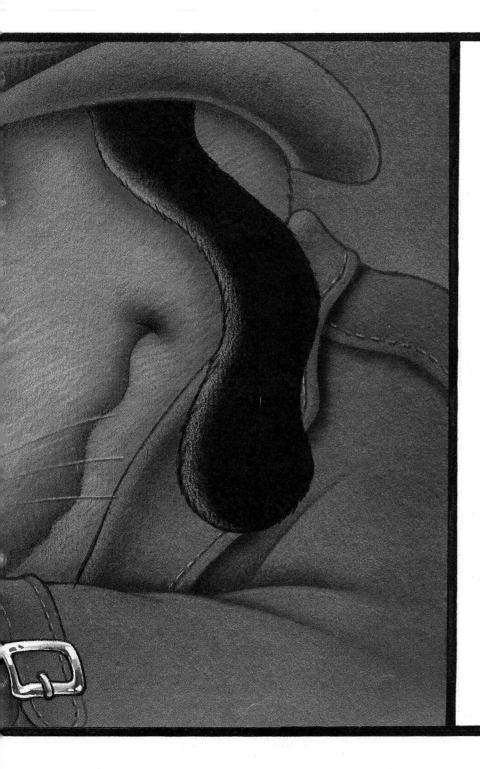

"Detective Dog! I found something over here!" announced Craig Frog.

Detective Dog walked over to the jewelry case Craig was examining. He took out his magnifying glass and looked at the object.

"What is it, Detective Dog?" asked Jon Mouse.

"It looks like a piece of wax," said Detective Dog. He bent over and sniffed the wax. He came up gagging and coughing.

"Yuck! It's citronella wax!" sputtered Detective Dog.

"Hey! A new candle factory just opened in Closter. They make citronella candles. I went there just last week," said Craig Frog.

"Great! Then that's where we're headed next. Jon Mouse, bag that wax as evidence!" ordered Detective Dog.

Jon Mouse took out a pair of tweezers and put the wax sample in a plastic bag.

In less than half an hour, the team was standing outside the R&M Fruity Candle Company. Detective Dog tried the door.

"Locked! Ned Cat, if you please!" requested Detective Dog.

"Sure! Locks are my specialty," said Ned. He stepped up to the door, stuck his claw in the lock, and began his work. In a few moments, he stepped back and pushed the door open, only to find a brick wall on the other side.

18

"This is no ordinary candle factory!" said Detective Dog.

Matthew Spider, who had been quiet the entire time, stepped forward.

"I can get us over the wall!" said Matthew. He shot a thick strand of webbing over the wall. It stuck to the other side like glue to paper.

"Okay, now we can climb over," directed Matthew.

The team climbed up the webbing and dropped down on the other side of the wall. There they found a wooden door.

"This is getting rather monotonous," complained Jon.

"Here we go again!" said Ned, baring his claw.

"I have a better idea," said Craig, gesturing toward the ceiling. There was a key hanging from a hook. Craig leapt up and grabbed it.

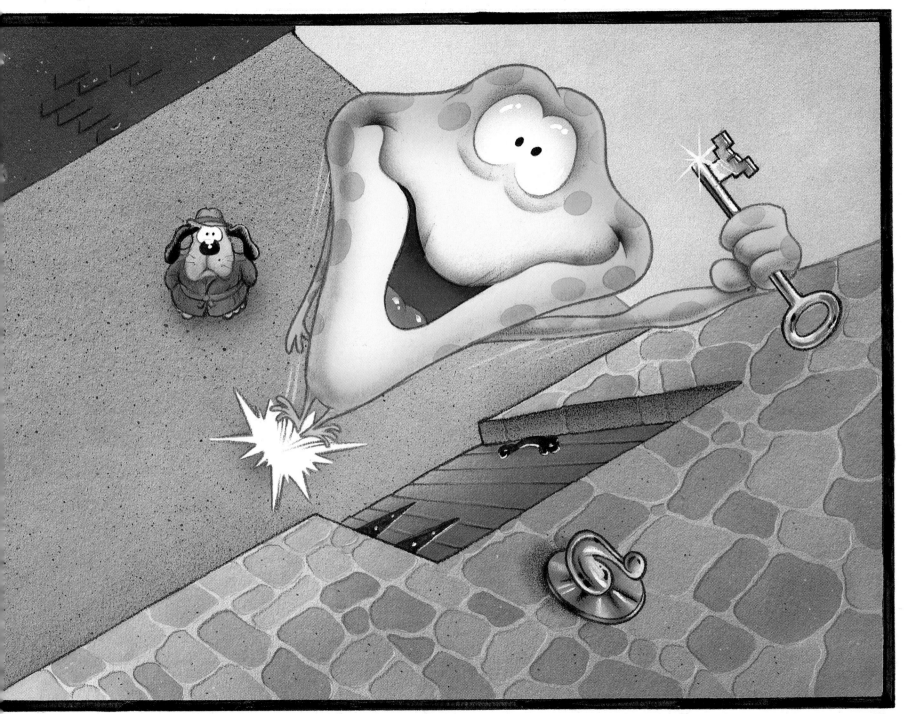

21

"There's something funny going on here," whispered Chris.

Craig shoved the key in the lock and turned it. Detective Dog opened the door, and the team stepped into a large, empty room.

"Something's wrong here!" exclaimed Detective Dog.

Just then, a loudspeaker blared a message to the team.

"So, you've found the final room? Well, I hate to break it to you, but this entire set-up has been one huge trap!"

As the loudspeaker cut off, the floor began to slide into the wall!

23

"Detective Dog, what's down there?" asked Chris.

Detective Dog looked down into the gap. "It's a giant cage! We'll be trapped!" he shouted.

"Not if I can help it!" said Jon Mouse. He suddenly ran over to a small, plain box that no one else had even noticed and opened it.

"Let's see . . . should I pull the red wire or the blue wire?" wondered Jon Mouse.

"Hurry! We can't hold on to the floor much longer!" yelled Craig Frog.

Jon Mouse thought for another moment, then yanked out both the red and blue wires. Instantly, the floor stopped in its tracks!

25

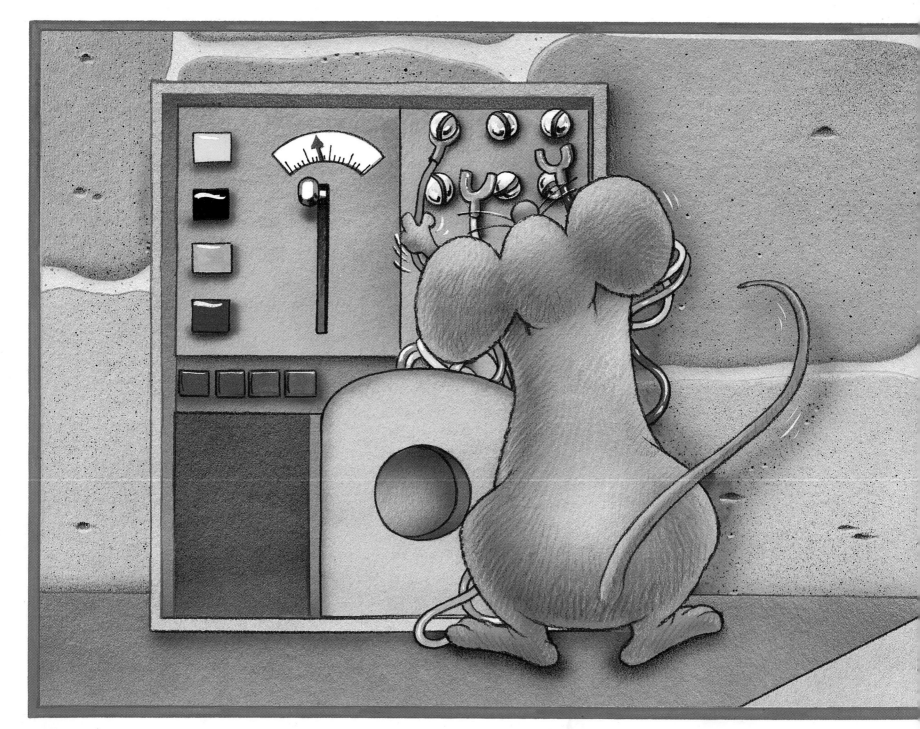

"Hmmm . . . that actually worked! Now, let's try this!" said Jon Mouse. He took the wires and stuck them into the opposite sockets. The floor slid back into place, and a door on the other side sprang open, revealing a closet full of stolen jewelry and hollowed-out citronella candles!

Detective Dog walked into the room and noticed a small booklet under a candle.

"It's Rocky Fruit Bat's passport! And there's an action plan attached to it explaining the whole scheme to smuggle these jewels to Europe!" said Detective Dog.

"Rocky Fruit Bat? As in Rocky and Muggsy Fruit Bat, the notorious smuggling brothers?" asked Chris Duck.

"Well, it would make sense. Guys, I believe we've solved this mystery!" said Detective Dog, triumphantly.

"And between the passport and the jewels, we have enough evidence to bring the two of them to justice," announced Jon Mouse.

The team slapped each other high fives.

29

30

The next day, Rocky and Muggsy were captured outside Philadelphia and brought back to New Jersey's Bergen County Jail. The brothers were charged with resisting arrest and jewelry theft.

Once again, the Detective Dog Team had triumphed.

CASE CLOSED

Jonathan V. Cann, author of **The Case of the Crooked Candles**, was a sixth grader in an honors class at Brookside Elementary School when he won the 1996 Publish-a-Book™ Contest, but he spent the first six years of his school career at Berkeley Elementary. It was there in second grade that he wrote his first Detective Dog story, as a creative writing assignment. Since then, he has continued to write stories, both in longhand and on computer.

Jonathan lives in Westwood, New Jersey, with his mother, Joan, his father, Ted, and his nine-year-old sister, Meredith.

When he isn't writing stories, Jonathan enjoys playing video games, computer games, and basketball; visiting with family and friends; and collecting all kinds of strange yet wonderful things.

The twenty honorable-mention winners in the **1996 Raintree/Steck-Vaughn Publish-a-Book™ Contest** were Amy Anderson, Joyce Kilmer School, Milltown, New Jersey; Meghan Codd, Riffenburgh Elementary School, Fort Collins, Colorado; Jonathan Cantwell, Ramblewood Elementary School, Coral Springs, Florida; Christopher Riedel, Haycock Elementary School, Falls Church, Virginia; Jonathan Jans, Jack Hille School, Oak Forest, Illinois; Kevin P. Barry, John Pettibone School, New Milford, Connecticut; Hiram Lew, St. Thomas Apostle School, San Francisco, California; Becky Kuplin, Sussex County Eastern District Library, Franklin, New Jersey; Amanda Marchetti, St. Joseph Memorial School, Hazleton, Pennsylvania; Julia K. Corley, Ruby Ray Swift Elementary School, Arlington, Texas; Sally Rees, Richards Elementary School, Whitefish Bay, Wisconsin; Katherine Connors, Haycock Elementary School, Falls Church, Virginia; Amanda R. Simpson, Mitchell Elementary School, Mitchell, Nebraska; Sarah Wexelbaum, Pine Crest School, Boca Raton, Florida; Matthew Ports, Hope Christian School, Albuquerque, New Mexico; Bridget Taylor, St. Anne's School, Bethlehem, Pennsylvania; Hillary Birtley, Clark Elementary School, St. Louis, Missouri; Chris Morin, Boulan Park Middle School, Troy, Michigan; Lauren Ferris, St. Vincent's Elementary School, Petaluma, California; Rula Assi, Juniper School, Escondido, California.

Jean Pidgeon lives in Maryland, on Bodkin Creek, along Chesapeake Bay. She works at Historic Savage Mill, a renovated cotton mill that is now an antique and arts center. She loves every minute she spends making her living illustrating children's books and is thankful for all the wonderful writers who create a need for her work. Jean also illustrated other Raintree/Steck-Vaughn Publish-a-Book™ Contest winners including *Friends Afloat (1992)* and *Harvey's Wish (1994)*.